EVERYTHING SPORTS

EVERYTHING
VOLLEYBALL

CORBU STATHES

SportsZone

An Imprint of Abdo Publishing
abdobooks.com

abdobooks.com

Published by Abdo Publishing, a division of ABDO, PO Box 398166, Minneapolis, Minnesota 55439. Copyright © 2025 by Abdo Consulting Group, Inc. International copyrights reserved in all countries. No part of this book may be reproduced in any form without written permission from the publisher. SportsZone™ is a trademark and logo of Abdo Publishing.

Printed in China.
052024
092024

Cover Photos: Shutterstock Images (background); David Buono/Icon Sportswire/AP Images (foreground)
Interior Photos: Steven Branscombe/Getty Images Sport/Getty Images, 4–5; Michelle L. Mitchell/The News Virginian/AP Images, 6–7; Hulton Archive/Getty Images, 8–9; AP Images, 10; Bain News Service/Library of Congress, 11; Raphael Dias/Getty Images Sport/Getty Images, 13; Mathilda Ahlberg/Bildbyran/Sipa USA/AP Images, 14–15; Rodolfo Buhrer/Eurasia Sport Images/Getty Images Sport/Getty Images, 16–17; Stephen Lew/Cal Sport Media/AP Images, 19; Richard A. Brooks/AFP/Getty Images, 20–21; Abdulhamid Hosbas/Anadolu/Getty Images, 22–23; Nikos Frazier/Omaha World-Herald/AP Images, 25; Jeff Roberson/AP Images, 26–27; Jacob Snow/Icon Sportswire/Getty Images, 29; Massimo Insabato/Mondadori Portfolio/Sipa USA/AP Images, 30–31; Bob Galbraith/AP Images, 32–33; Markus Boesch/Allsport/Getty Images Sport/Getty Images, 34; Justin Tafoya/NCAA Photos/Getty Images, 36–37; Jamie Schwaberow/NCAA Photos/Getty Images, 39; Victor Decolongon/Getty Images Sport/Getty Images, 41; Daugherty/AP Images, 42–43; Toru Hanai/Getty Images Sport/Getty Images, 44; Zhu Zheng/Xinhua News Agency/Getty Images, 46–47; Ian Waldie/Getty Images Sport/Getty Images, 48–49; Christopher Morris/Corbis Sport/Getty Images, 50; Hristo Rusev/NurPhoto/Getty Images, 52–53; Aldara Zarraoa/Getty Images Sport/Getty Images, 55; Andre Kang/GDA Photo/AP Images, 56–57; Carl De Souza/AFP/Getty Images, 58; Chris O'Meara/AP Images, 61

Editor: Charlie Beattie
Series Designer: Karli Kruse

Library of Congress Control Number: 2023949386
Publisher's Cataloging-in-Publication Data
Names: Stathes, Corbu, author.
Title: Everything volleyball / by Corbu Stathes
Description: Minneapolis, Minnesota: Abdo Publishing, 2025 | Series: Everything sports | Includes online resources and index.
Identifiers: ISBN 9781098293628 (lib. bdg.) | ISBN 9798384912897 (ebook)
Subjects: LCSH: Volleyball--Juvenile literature. | Volleyball players--Juvenile literature. | Volleyball coaches--Juvenile literature. | Volleyball injuries--Juvenile literature. | Beach volleyball--Juvenile literature. | Volleyball--Training--Juvenile literature. | Volleyball--Records--Juvenile literature. | Sports--Juvenile literature.
Classification: DDC 796.325--dc23

TABLE OF CONTENTS

CHAPTER ONE

IN THE ARENA

With a loud smack, the ball is put into play. It screams over the net. A diving dig by the libero prevents the serve from hitting the ground. The ball is lofted toward the setter, who pops it into the air with precision. With another loud smack, the outside hitter hammers it down on the other side of the court. Power, agility, and speed are all on display every day on the volleyball court.

That's what the largest crowd ever to watch a women's sporting event came to see. On August 30, 2023, more than 92,000 people flooded Memorial Stadium at the University of Nebraska. They weren't there to see the famed Cornhuskers football team. Instead, the school's women's volleyball team was using the massive stadium to host the University of Nebraska Omaha.

Nebraska's Harper Murray starts a point with a jump serve against Nebraska Omaha on August 30, 2023.

The Huskers football team had played many important games at Memorial Stadium. Yet none had as many fans. The previous world record for a crowd at a women's sporting event was set in 2022. A soccer match between European powers FC Barcelona and VfL Wolfsburg drew 91,648 fans. Meanwhile, the biggest crowd to see a women's college volleyball match had been 18,755, when Nebraska fell to Wisconsin in the 2021 national title game.

Volleyball dates back to the late 1800s. It is more popular today than ever. From the court to the sand, from kids to the pros, from barbecues to the Olympics, volleyball is thriving on many levels. A report released in 2022 showed it was the second-fastest growing sport among high school girls in the United States over the previous 20 years. And the big crowds keep coming out. In 2023, the college women's volleyball final between Texas and Nebraska drew 19,727 fans in the arena. Another 1.7 million viewers watched on television. That set a record for a college volleyball match.

More than 520,000 high school students in the United States competed in volleyball during the 2021–22 school year.

CHAPTER TWO

A NEW SPORT

In 1895, William G. Morgan was working at a Young Men's Christian Association (YMCA) in Massachusetts. Basketball had been invented a few years earlier, also in Massachusetts. But the sport proved to be too strenuous for older people to play. Morgan borrowed from other sports to create a more relaxing sport for older members. He started with a basketball. He got the idea of a net from tennis. He liked how handball players could use their hands to hit the ball. And he decided to mimic the idea of innings from baseball, in which only one team could score at a time.

Morgan presented his new game at the YMCA Physical Directors Conference in 1896. The directors liked the idea. Before long, and with the help of the YMCA's presence around the world, Morgan's new game began spreading.

Volleyball spread first to Canada in the early 1900s, then later around the world.

US Army soldiers helped popularize volleyball globally. They were issued balls and nets to play on bases stationed around the world, and local people soon picked up on the game they were playing.

The sport looked very different than it does today. The court was smaller. The net was lower. There was no limit to how many people could be on each side. Players could also hit the ball an unlimited number of times before sending it over the net. If a serve wasn't going to make it over the net, a teammate could help it along. In a nod to baseball, each game was nine innings long. And just as a baseball team gets three outs in an inning, early volleyball rules stated that each team served three times per inning.

Albert Goodwill Spalding was a former baseball player who became rich making sporting goods.

In 1900, a local sporting goods manufacturer named Albert Goodwill Spalding created a ball specific to the sport. The lighter, smaller ball created a faster game. That allowed volleyball to grow into the dynamic game fans know today.

During the early years, different playing styles emerged in different parts of the world. In 1916, the YMCA and the National Collegiate Athletics Association (NCAA) published a set of rules for the United States. Global rules didn't come until 1947. The new set of rules helped create a uniform game.

Now, volleyball is played by more than 800 million people worldwide. It has been adapted to the sand as beach volleyball. Sitting volleyball was invented in 1956 to give people with disabilities a chance to play. That version of the sport is now a part of the Paralympic Games. No matter which version of volleyball people play, it's one of the most popular team sports in the world.

Iran, *in white*, and Bosnia-Herzegovina, *in blue*, combined to win all nine Olympic gold medals in sitting volleyball between 1988 and 2021.

CHAPTER THREE

BASIC RULES

The objective of volleyball is simple. Each team tries to prevent the ball from hitting the ground on its side of the net. If the ball lands on the floor, the other team is awarded a point.

The net divides the court in half. The height of the net varies depending on the age of the players. At the highest levels, it's 7 feet, 11 5/8 inches (2.4 m) tall for men and 7 feet, 4 1/8 inches (2.2 m) for women. Each team has the same number of players. For indoor volleyball there are six players per side. The players begin each point in specific areas of the court. Beach volleyball can be played with four players on a team, but most high-level competitions are played with two per side. Players must stay on their own side of the net.

Because of the small size of the court, volleyball is easy to set up inside an existing gym.

With only two players per side, beach volleyball points tend to be quick and action-packed.

A rally is started when the ball is put into play by a serve. The serve must clear the net, or else the opponent gets a point. Once the ball is over the net, each team has three hits to return it to the other side. One way to win the rally and earn a point is for a team to get the ball to hit the ground on the opponent's side. A team can also earn a point if the opponent hits the ball out of bounds or fails to get the ball over the net in three hits. Whichever team scores the point gets to serve next. When the serve changes teams, each team must rotate its players one position on the court.

Indoor volleyball has six areas on the court, three in the front row and three in the back. The rows are separated by the 10-foot line. Each row has a left, middle, and right. After serving from the back right position, a player rotates clockwise one spot. Players who start in the back row cannot cross the 10-foot line to hit a ball. However, a player

WHEN SCORING WASN'T EASY

Under volleyball's original scoring system, only the serving team could earn a point. If the defending team won a rally, it took over the serve but did not earn a point. Under that system, games were usually played to 15. They also could last a long time. In 1999, USA Volleyball changed to rally scoring. That means a team earns a point on every rally. It made the set times much more consistent.

can jump and land over the 10-foot line as long as they take off from behind the line.

Volleyball can be played anywhere there's a net. However, standard court sizes are used for organized matches. An indoor volleyball court size is 29.5 feet (9 m) wide by 59.5 feet (18 m) long. A beach volleyball court is smaller, at 26.25 feet (8 m) wide and 52.5 feet (16 m) long.

A volleyball match is made up of sets. In indoor volleyball, a team needs to win three sets to win the match. At most levels, the first team to reach 25 points wins the set. But there is one catch. The team has to be winning by two points when they reach 25. If they aren't, play continues until one team takes a two-point lead. Beach volleyball is played to 21 points in a best-of-three-sets format. In both versions of the sport, if a match is tied going into the final set, that set is played to 15 points.

Volleyball players spend hours on the practice court to perfect the timing of their offensive attacks.

CHAPTER FOUR

FROM SERVE TO SPIKE

To win points in volleyball, it's important to know the basic moves. Each rally starts with the serve. Standing behind the end line, the server must hit the ball over the net. This can only be done with one hand, but it can be underhand or overhand. A good serve is hard for the opponent to return. A serve that is not returned is called an ace.

Once the ball is over the net, teams generally use all three hits to give themselves the best opportunity for a point. These three hits are usually the reception, the set, and the attack. These are sometimes referred to as the bump, set, and spike.

The first touch after the serve is called the reception. The player receiving the ball often does so by clasping their hands together with their arms in the shape of a V. They use their forearms to hit the ball. Ideally this is a pass to another teammate, preferably the setter.

Adis Lagumdžija of Turkey, *top,* watches his serve clear the net while playing in a 2023 match.

Due to the speed of volleyball, digging the ball sometimes takes an all-out effort.

Not all receptions are so simple, though. A dig is when a player is able to prevent an attack from hitting the floor with any part of their body. When a defender dives and gets a hand between the ball and floor at the last second to keep the point alive, it's called a pancake. So long as they can keep the ball in the air long enough for a teammate to reach it, the play stays alive.

Next comes the set. This overhead pass is an attempt to put the attacker in the best possible position to spike the ball over the net. Ideally, a setter uses the fingertips on both of their hands to lob the ball up to a teammate.

The attack is any hit that goes over the net toward the opponent. Teams can attack in different ways. But one of volleyball's most common attacks, and most exciting plays, is a spike. That's when a player soars through the air and slams the ball down with power. This attack comes from near the net with a strong, one-handed hit down toward the court. If the ball hits the floor after the attack, it's called a kill. Setters often

BOMBS AWAY

The use of the set and spike in volleyball originated in the Philippines in the 1920s. This new offensive strategy became known as "bomba," or "the Filipino bomb." It earned those nicknames because of how fast the ball would travel as it landed in the opponent's side of the court.

try to be sneaky with their passes so opponents don't know who is going to hit the spike.

Defending teams usually try to stop a spike right away. They can do this by blocking the ball at the net. The blockers try to time their jumps and get their arms in the air so that the ball will bounce back to the attacker's side of the net. But if the ball gets past the blockers, it's up to a teammate to keep the ball in play with a dig or a pass.

When both teams are executing on both offense and defense, fans can witness some long, tense points. The longest rally in women's college volleyball history happened in 2014 between Arizona State University and the University of Utah. For 55 thrilling seconds, the Sun Devils and Utes sent the ball over the net a total of 17 times. The highlight of the rally was a brilliant save from Arizona State's Macey Gardner, as she managed to keep the point alive from several feet behind the baseline. Eventually, Arizona State won the point when Utah blocked Sun Devils' outside hitter BreElle Bailey's spike attempt, but the ball landed out of bounds.

Two blockers for Arkansas set up during a match against Kentucky in 2023.

CHAPTER FIVE

TAKE YOUR PLACES

In indoor volleyball, each of the six players on a side is assigned a spot on the court to begin a rally. Only once the ball is in the air can a player move away from their assigned spot. This allows players to take on specific positions and specialties.

The setter is the quarterback of the offense. They are responsible for taking the first pass and launching an attack for a teammate. The setter decides who to feed the ball to by reading the opponent's defense. A good setter usually stays on the court through all six rotations.

Outside hitters and opposite hitters are typically a team's primary attackers. That's because setting to the outside is easiest for a setter. The outside hitter plays from the left side of the court. They are usually the best attacker on a team.

A serve starts every volleyball point.

The opposite hitter plays on the right side of the court. Both players are also expected to be strong blockers and able to play defense while in the back row.

The team's tallest player is usually put at the middle blocker position. As the name suggests, the middle blocker is mostly responsible for defending the middle third of the court. They may also be good at attacking, but making a set to the middle can be hard. That means opportunities for kills are rare. Middle blockers are most valuable in the front row, so teams often sub them out when they rotate to the back.

The libero often takes the place of the middle blocker. Liberos are easy to spot because they wear a different colored jersey from the rest of the team. They are in the game for their defensive abilities. Liberos are not allowed to attack the ball from above the net. Substitution rules also don't apply to a libero.

The libero position was created for international play in 1998. Colleges in the United States adopted the position four years later.

Wilfredo León of Poland set a record with 13 aces in a 2021 match.

However, they have to stay in the back row. Most defensive specialists are considered better passers than liberos. A libero's main goal is just to keep the ball alive. A defensive specialist does that as well. But instead of just making contact on their dig, they are looking to turn it into a pass that can start a solid attack.

A defensive specialist is different from a libero. They do have to follow substitution rules, so they are usually only in for the three back-row rotations. They also wear the same-colored jersey as the rest of their teammates.

If a player has a strong serve, they may become a serving specialist. They are in only for the serving rotation. They enter in place of a player who is not very good at serving but is good at other parts of the game.

CHAPTER SIX

TAKE IT OUTSIDE

A new game was born on the sandy beaches of California in the 1930s. The culture of beach volleyball was an important part of the sport. It began as more of a casual activity rather than a competition. Players talked about it having a family atmosphere. It was all about being laid-back, making friends, and playing the game they loved. Many of those elements have remained even as the sport has increased its worldwide profile.

One of the early faces of beach volleyball was Christopher "Sinjin" Smith. Crowds were tiny when Smith first started winning beach tournaments in the late 1970s. Fans that were there didn't even have bleachers to sit on. They had to stand, sit, or kneel in the sand. By the time Smith won his

Beach volleyball was first included in the Olympics as a demonstration sport at the 1992 Games in Barcelona, Spain. Sinjin Smith and partner Randy Stoklos of Team USA won the tournament.

Gabby Reece played professional beach volleyball from 1992 to 2000.

last title 16 years later, matches were on TV and the stands were packed.

Smith became known as the "King of the Beach." He and his partner Randy Stoklos won more professional beach tournaments than anyone else. His popularity led to appearances in TV shows, movies, and even a video game.

Gabby Reece was one of beach volleyball's biggest celebrities in the 1990s. After playing at Florida State University, she became a professional with the Women's Beach Volleyball League. She led the league in kills four consecutive years. She also led a four-person team to the title at the first-ever Beach Volleyball World Championships in 1997. Reece's fame led to many endorsement opportunities. She was one of the first spokespeople for Nike from a non-traditional sport. She even designed a popular shoe for the company.

The love for beach volleyball grew around the world It really took root in Brazil. The South American country has more than 2,000 beaches on its 4,650 miles (7,483 km) of coastline, so there are plenty of opportunities to play. It became the second most popular sport in the country, behind only soccer. Soon Brazil became an Olympic powerhouse. Beach volleyball was introduced to the Summer Games in 1996. A men's or women's Brazilian team won a medal in the sport at each of the first six Games.

Pro tours grew both internationally and in the United States. In 1997, the Fédération Internationale de Volleyball (FIVB) held its first official World Championships. They are held every other year. Brazil has dominated in that tournament, too, with 13 gold medals (seven men's and six women's) through 2023. The first NCAA title in women's beach volleyball was awarded in 2016. The University of Southern California (USC) won five of the first seven titles.

Nicole Nourse and the USC Trojans celebrated their 2021 national championship in beach volleyball by jumping in the nearby ocean in Gulf Shores, Alabama.

CHAPTER SEVEN

A DEGREE HIGHER

The NCAA first sanctioned women's college volleyball in 1981. Since then, two schools have dominated the sport. Through 2023, the Stanford Cardinal had won nine championships. They had appeared in the championship match 17 times. Both of those totals led all college teams. In 2023, the Cardinal appeared in their 42nd straight NCAA tournament.

Stanford's strength comes in part from the outstanding players it recruits. Many have also found success at the Olympic level. Between 1988 and 2020, every US Olympic indoor team had at least one former Stanford star on its roster. Middle blocker Foluke Akinradewo Gunderson helped the US women win their first indoor volleyball gold medal in 2021.

That success has carried over to the beach too. All four of the gold medals the United States has won in Olympic women's beach volleyball have included a former Stanford player. Kerri Walsh Jennings won three golds. Alix Klineman took home her first gold in at the Tokyo Olympics in 2021.

Penn State was just behind Stanford with seven NCAA titles. But no team can match Penn State's run of four consecutive NCAA titles from 2007 to 2010. The Nittany Lions

The Stanford Cardinal women celebrated their ninth NCAA championship in 2019. The school won its first in 1992.

topped Stanford in the title game each of the first two years of that streak.

Maybe even more impressive was Penn State's winning streak during that span. The Nittany Lions won an NCAA record 109 straight matches. In 2008, they didn't lose a match. They didn't even lose a single set in the regular season. They lost only two sets in the NCAA tournament.

Men's college volleyball is less popular than the women's game. While there are 334 Division I women's programs, only 23 Division I schools field a men's team. The University of California, Los Angeles (UCLA) has dominated the men's sport. The Bruins won their 20th national championship in 2023. UCLA is just one of many California schools that rule men's volleyball. Pepperdine has five titles, while USC and the University of California, Irvine have four each.

In addition to the Penn State women's team dominating from 2007 to 2010, the school's men's team also won the 2008 national championship.

CHAPTER EIGHT

INDOOR OLYMPIANS

Volleyball may have been invented in the United States, but Team USA was not an Olympic power right away. The first Olympic volleyball tournaments were held at the 1964 Games in Tokyo, Japan. But a US team didn't even earn a medal until 1984. That year, the men's team took home gold and the women's team won silver in Los Angeles.

Karch Kiraly was a star on that 1984 men's team. The then 23-year-old was just starting a long, successful career in the sport. He won three NCAA titles at UCLA. He also won 148 beach tournaments. And he earned another Olympic gold medal in indoor volleyball at the 1988 Games in Seoul, South Korea. Kiraly then won gold in beach volleyball in the 1996 Olympics in Atlanta. FIVB named him the greatest volleyball player of the 20th century.

Members of Team USA celebrate on the medal stand after winning gold at the 1984 Olympics.

Karch Kiraly speaks to the US women's team during a timeout at the Tokyo Olympics in 2021.

Though the US women were often competitive in major tournaments, the Olympic gold medal eluded them for many years. The US women won bronze in 1992. Then they missed out on medals at the next three Olympic Games. They reached the gold-medal match in 2008 and 2012 but lost to Brazil both times. The Americans settled for bronze again in 2016.

Finally, in 2021 at the Games in Tokyo, Team USA put it all together. The US women were dominant in pool play, losing just one match. They were even better in the medal round. The United States didn't lose a single set on its way to the gold-medal match.

Brazil once again stood in the United States' way for the top spot on the medal stand. The Brazilian team hadn't ost a match in the entire tournament. But the US women weren't intimidated. They swept the Brazilians and finally got to

TOKYO, 1964

Volleyball was the first women's team sport included in the Olympic Games. The sport was big in Japan, so the 1964 Tokyo Games were a fitting site for the first Olympic tournament. The host team had a wildly popular group of athletes who captured the imagination of the entire country. The team had not lost in four years entering the tournament. In the gold-medal match, they faced the last team to have beaten them, the Soviet Union. Japan won in straight sets as an estimated 80 percent of the country watched on TV.

wear the gold medals around their necks. The coach for the women's team was none other than Karch Kiraly.

Through the 2020 Olympics, three countries had taken home six medals each in men's volleyball. Brazil had three golds and three silvers. The Soviet Union won three golds, two silvers, and a bronze. Italy had three silvers and three bronze. China, Japan, the Soviet Union, and the United States have all won at least six medals on the women's side. Cuba also won three straight gold medals between 1992 and 2000.

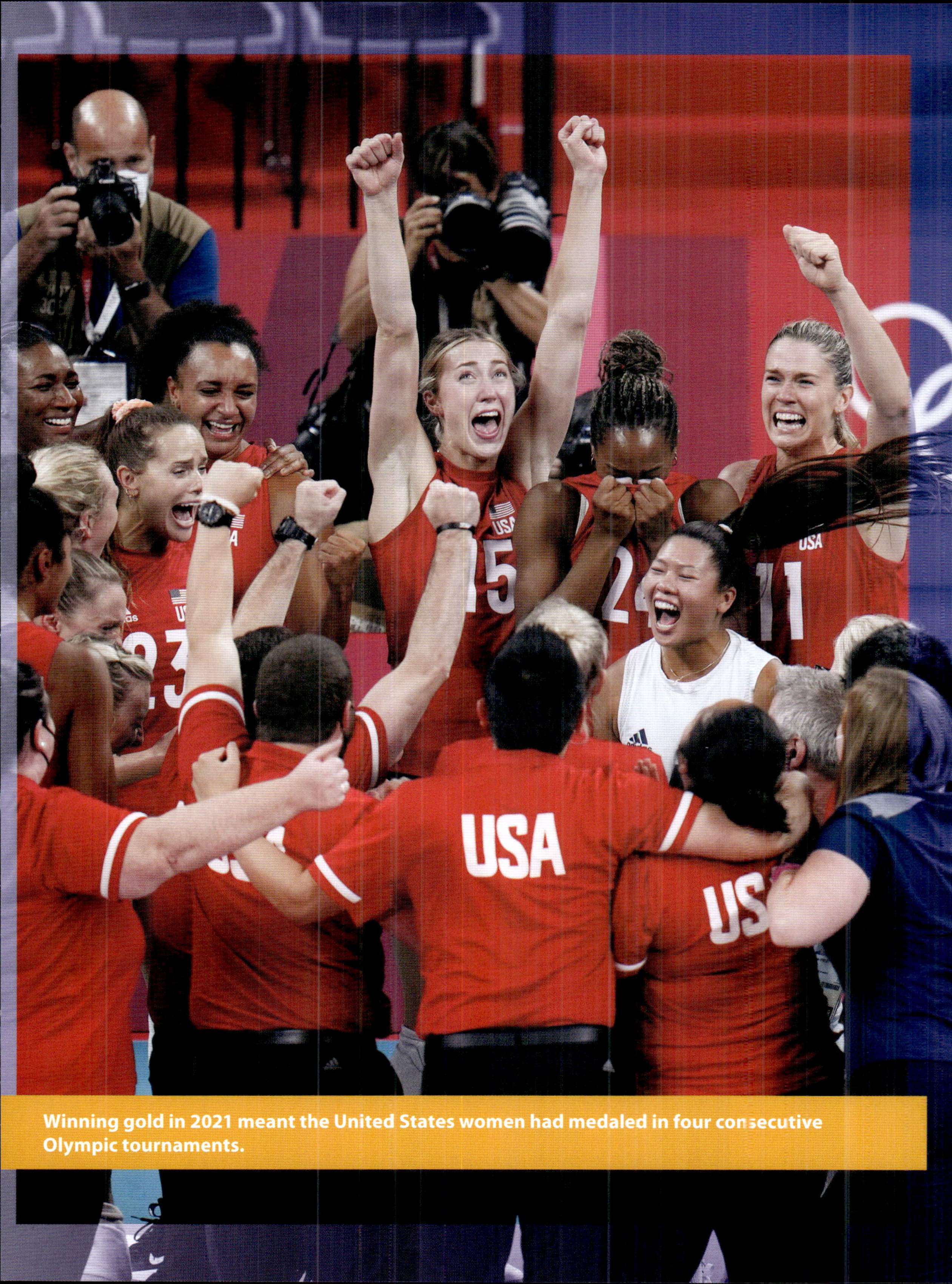

Winning gold in 2021 meant the United States women had medaled in four consecutive Olympic tournaments.

OLYMPIC SAND

Beach volleyball was introduced at the Olympics as a demonstration sport at the 1992 Games. Four years later, it became a full sport. No Americans medaled in either the 1996 or 2000 competitions. But in 2004, the team of Misty May-Treanor and Kerri Walsh Jennings took the tournament by storm.

Both had appeared in the Olympics before 2004. May-Treanor was in the beach volleyball tournament, and Walsh Jennings was on the US indoor team for the 2000 Games. They teamed up for beach volleyball on the professional circuit in 2001. The pair meshed quickly, and were ranked number one in the world by 2002. In 2003, they won 90 straight matches, a record at the time.

Misty May-Treanor, *left*, and Kerri Walsh Jennings, *right*, celebrate on the medal stand after winning gold at the 2004 Olympics.

May-Treanor and Walsh Jennings carried that success over to the 2004 Olympics. They didn't lose a set on their way to the gold medal. It was the first gold for a US women's beach volleyball duo. It wouldn't be their last.

May-Treanor goes up for a spike at the 2012 Games in London, England.

The pair didn't lose a set in the 2008 Games either. The gold-medal match was a challenge, though. The Olympics were held in Beijing, China, that year, and May-Treanor and Walsh Jennings faced a team from China in the final. They beat Tian Jia and Wang Jie in a steady rain to win their second straight gold.

Then, in 2012 May-Treanor and Walsh Jennings became the first beach volleyball team to win three Olympic gold medals. They did so again in dominant fashion, losing just one set in seven matches. In their three Olympic appearances together, May-Treanor and Walsh Jennings went 21–0 in matches and 42–1 in sets against the best players in the world. After May-Treanor retired, Walsh Jennings competed in one more Olympics in 2016 with partner April Ross. They earned a bronze medal in Rio de Janeiro, Brazil.

CHAPTER TEN

WORLD TOURNAMENTS

The best teams in the world don't wait for the Olympics to square off. FIVB puts together many competitions for national teams of all ages. And they take place all over the world.

FIVB was formed in 1947 in Paris, France, to create standardized rules and unify the sport. Prior to that, the rules were slightly different in every part of the world. Once everyone was playing by the same rules, world championships could be held.

Currently there is a four-year rotation of global events for indoor volleyball. The World Cup, the World Championships, and regional events such as the Asian Games and Pan American Games take place in non-Olympic years. There are also annual events for countries to compete in, including the Nations League and the Challenger Cup.

French hitter Kevin Le Roux prepares for a spike at the first-ever Nations League tournament, which was held in 2018. France reached the final before losing to Russia.

PROFESSIONAL VOLLEYBALL

College volleyball has grown into a major sport in the United States. Professional indoor volleyball hasn't had the same success. But many countries around the world are home to popular men's and women's professional leagues. Many US players head to countries such as Brazil and Italy to continue their pro careers.

The first beach volleyball World Championships were held in 1997. The event is held every other year. Between the World Championships, beach players also have opportunities to play in professional tournaments. The Association of Volleyball Professionals tour has been around since 1983. The FIVB World Tour began in 1989 for men and 1992 for women. That tour was replaced by the Volleyball World Beach Pro Tour in 2022. These professional beach tournaments are popular, with big crowds at many stops. The teams are made up of some of the best players in the world.

The Volleyball World Beach Pro Tour held events in 27 countries in 2023.

CHAPTER ELEVEN

TIPS FOR YOUNG PLAYERS

It takes a lot of practice to become good at volleyball. But a full team isn't necessary to hone one's skills. Practicing alone or with a friend can be valuable. When training alone, a player can hit a ball against a wall above where the net would be. When the ball bounces back, they can try to pass it and set it to themselves before hitting it against the wall again. This exercise is called pepper. It can also be done with a partner. Instead of a wall, hit the ball to the other person. Pepper can help players read and anticipate where a ball is going to go.

Passing can be practiced by throwing the ball off the wall and then trying to bump it to a specific spot on the floor. Setting can be practiced the same way. Players should make sure to move around to get to the ball off the wall. Very rarely does a ball come right to a player in a match.

Learning proper techniques can take many hours of practice.

One of the most exciting plays in volleyball is the jump serve. Done right, it can be a powerful move and tough to return. This increases the chances for an ace.

There are two types of jump serves. One is the topspin serve. It has a lot of power behind it. In addition, the spin on the ball makes it dive down after crossing the net. The other jump serve is the float serve. The goal is to keep the ball from spinning. An object that doesn't spin moves unpredictably based on how the air is flowing around the court. A good float serve might suddenly change directions, which makes it tricky to handle.

Mastering the jump serve requires a lot of practice. There are six steps to the serve. They are the setup, toss, approach, jump, swing, and follow-through.

THAT'S FAST

The most powerful serve in men's volleyball traveled at more than 80 miles per hour (129 km/h). That would get the ball a speeding ticket on almost every highway. The record was set by Poland's Wilfredo León in 2023. One of his serves was clocked at 85.7 miles per hour (138 km/h). The women's record is held by Melissa Vargas of Turkey. She boomed a serve at 69.6 miles per hour (112 km/h) in a 2023 match.

The setup should begin far enough away from the end line that the approach won't lead the server onto the court. If a server steps on or over the back line during the serve, it's a fault and their team loses the point.

How far and how high the ball should be tossed depends on the type of serve being attempted. For a topspin serve, servers toss it up with the same hand used to hit the ball. A higher toss helps generate more power. When performing a float serve, use the opposite hand. The toss will be shorter and not as far in front of the server.

The approach consists of three steps after the ball is tossed into the air. A right-handed server's first step will be with the left foot. On the third step, they leap into the air to meet the ball. With the opposite arm out for balance, it looks a bit like a person holding a bow and arrow.

The jump and swing come next. On the swing, the ball should be hit at the top of one's reach. The hand should meet the middle of the ball as the opposite arm moves back toward the body.

The follow-through will help make the serve either spin or float. For a topspin serve, finish with a flick of the hand outward and down. Think of it like turning off a light switch with the entire hand. For a float, finish with the hand high and out in front, almost like the ball was being pushed toward the net.

Young servers need to be patient while they're learning. Practicing the steps individually helps to get a feel for them. When the individual steps are mastered, they can all be combined to form a powerful weapon on the court.

The best servers mix up serve type, speed, and location.

GLOSSARY

agility

The ability to move and shift quickly.

demonstration sport

A sport played at the Olympics solely to increase its popularity, and not for medals.

dig

In volleyball, a defensive play made to stop a ball from hitting the ground.

dynamic

Energetic and exciting; in sports, usually referring to an athlete with one or more outstanding skills.

dynasty

A team that has an extended period of success, usually winning multiple championships in the process.

elude

To avoid or get away from.

pool play

A portion of a tournament where teams play a set schedule of opponents in a round-robin format.

professional

A person who gets paid to perform.

rally

The series of actions two teams make to keep the ball in play.

recruit

Convince to join.

spokesperson

Someone who is paid to advertise a product or company.

standardize

To make consistent or regular.

Books

Flynn, Brendan. *Girls' Volleyball*. Abdo, 2022.

Price, Karen. *GOATs of Olympic Sports*. Abdo, 2022.

Stathes, Corbu. *Everything Baseball*. Abdo, 2025.

Online Resources

To learn more about volleyball, please visit **abdobooklinks.com** or scan this QR code. These links are routinely monitored and updated to provide the most current information available.

INDEX

About the Author

Corbu Stathes lives in Minnesota with his son. He works in college sports and loves researching and learning about new things.